DEVON
✠ WITCHCRAFT
and Folk Ways

Sarah Hewett

www.troybooks.co.uk

DEVON
✦ WITCHCRAFT ✦
and Folk Ways

© 2009 Troy Books Publishing
This selection, layout, cover design and new illustrations

First printed May 2009

ISBN 978-0-9561043-1-1

This selection from 'Nummits and Crummits' by Sarah Hewett
Originally published in 1900

All rights reserved.
No part of this publication may be reproduced, stored within a retrieval system or transmitted in any form or by any means, electronic, mechanical, photocopying, scanning, recording or otherwise, without the prior written permission of the publisher.

The contents of this book are presented as items of interest. The publisher accepts no responsibility for the results of their enactment or use. Readers are self responsible for their actions.

Published by Troy Books
www.troybooks.co.uk

Troy Books Publishing
PO.Box 304
Penzance, Cornwall
TR18 9EH
England

✣ CONTENTS ✣

Preface · 1

Charms · 2

   Charms to Heal · 5
   Charms for Protection · 13
   Curses - to Cast and to Counter · 17
   Love Divination Charms · 18
   Miscellaneous Charms · 21

Superstitions · 24

   All Hallowe'en Superstitions · 24
   Omens and Death Tokens · 33
   Marriage Ceremony Superstitions · 36
   Divination by the Bible · 38
   Clover and Ash - Leaf Superstition · 39
   About Salt · 40
   Oneiromancy · 40
   The Mistletoe Curse · 50
   Legend of the Glastonbury Thorn · 51
   The Chagford Pixies · 51
   The Ghost of the Black-Dog · 52
   Superstitions Attached to Church Bells · 54
   The Seventh Son · 55
   Sunday · 55

Things Lucky and Unlucky　　　　　　　　　　　56

    It is Lucky...　　　　　　　　　　　　　　56
    It is Unlucky...　　　　　　　　　　　　　59
    Unlucky Days　　　　　　　　　　　　　67

Customs　　　　　　　　　　　　　　　　　68

    The Hobby Horse　　　　　　　　　　　68
    May Day　　　　　　　　　　　　　　　69
    The Ashen Faggot　　　　　　　　　　　71
    A Harvest Custom　　　　　　　　　　　71
    The Divining Rod　　　　　　　　　　　74

Weather Lore and Wise Saws　　　　　　　　75

    Signs of Rain as Predicted by the Habits of Birds　　90
    and Animals

Resources　　　　　　　　　　　　　　　　94

George Martin.

✧ PREFACE ✧

This little book is made up of a few crumbs from the repositories of many Devonshire friends, to whom grateful thanks are tendered for their untiring helpfulness in supplying so much that is quaint and interesting.

The miscellaneous scraps here gathered show but inadequately the humorous characteristics of our Devonshire folk, their dialect, and as some like to call it, "jargon" as drawn by themselves. They illustrate what the people actually believe in, say and do and show the general trend of their minds. Their belief in the supernatural is unbounded. Neither age, social position, nor culture makes much difference: one and all are more or less wedded to the superstitions, beliefs and traditions of their ancestors.

It is impossible to say from whom they arrived, as hundreds of newspaper and other cuttings came to hand anonymously and being very precious morsels were reproduced. To each and all contributors most grateful thanks are given.

SARAH HEWETT.

Tiverton, Devon,
July 1899.

✣ CHARMS ✣

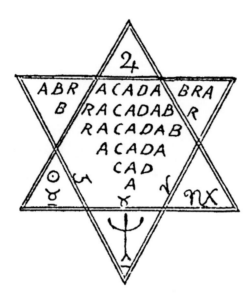

Where is the Necromancer? Let him bring his
Treasury of charms, rich syrups, herbs
Gathered in eclipse: or when shooting stars
Sow earth with pearls; or, let him call his sprites
Till the air thickens, and the golden noon
Smote by his wings, is turned to sudden midnight.
- Croly

West Country people generally, and Devonians in particular, are exceedingly superstitious, in spite of all that has been done for them in the way of higher education, and the enlightening influence of the press. Dwellers in the hilly parts of Devon, on Dartmoor and Exmoor, and in the villages bordering upon them, are as deeply imbued with faith in witches, as their forefathers were in the days when Alfred was king. According to tradition there are three kinds of witches.

The Black Witch, who is of an intensely malignant nature, and responsible for all the ills that flesh is heir to.

The White Witch, of an opposite nature, is always willing, for certain pecuniary considerations, to dispense charms and philtres, to cancel the evil of the other.

The Grey Witch is the worst of all, for she possesses the double power of either "overlooking" or "releasing".

In cases of sickness, distress, or adversity, persons at the present time (A.D. 1898) make long expensive journeys to consult the white witch, and to gain relief by her (or his) aid.

The surest method of escaping the influence of the evil eye, is to draw blood from the person of the witch. Shakespeare, in Henry III, says:

"Devil or devil's dam, I'll conjure thee:
Blood will I draw. Thou art a witch."

A country man told me recently that he had "raped old mother Tapp's arm with a great rusty nail two or three times," said he.

The mode of applying charms and medicaments has been handed down to us from the remotest ages. The witch doctor cured through the imagination. "Conceit will kill and conceit will cure," said a celebrated Harley Street physician to a medical student who one day applied to him for advice. It certainly is the case with regard to talismans. Playing on a patient's will and feelings, has stronger power in curing diseases than we are inclined to credit. To the powerful influence of strong-minded, unscrupulous persons over those of weaker constitution may be attributed the success of the nostrums prescribed. Added to the physical presence of the charm, the hypnotic persuasion of the operator compels the patient to believe that a cure has been effected through the charm.

Pinches of powdered plants, scraps of inscribed vellum, dried limbs of loathsome reptiles, juices of poisonous herbs, blood, excrements, and gruesome compositions all blend together to make up the witch's charms. Who among the weak in mind, the uneducated, and the frivolous could resist falling a victim to the seductive attraction of a talisman, whose virtues would secure health, wealth and happiness? Much of a witch's success depended on the unremitting persuasive force she exerted on her patients to stimulate them to believe implicitly in her. This once attained, her influence became unlimited. The degree of strength exerted affected the progress of convalescence. For mercenary reasons the witch took care that a cure was not too quickly brought about.

I have interviewed many a believer in the efficacy of charms, and from them obtained curious examples of miscellaneous articles claiming miraculous powers to heal. Besides the sale of charms the white witch cures diseases by "striking" and blessing. The following are a few examples.

✵ Charms to Heal ✵

TO CURE SKIN DISEASE

Place the poison found in a toad's head in a leathern bag one inch square; enclose this in a white silk bag, tie it round the neck, allowing the bag to lie on the pit of the stomach. On the third day the patient will be sick. Remove and bury the bag. As it rots so will the patient get well.

TO REMOVE WARTS

Take an eel and cut off the head. Rub the warts with the blood of the head. Then bury the head in the ground. When the head is rotten the warts fall off.

ANOTHER CURE FOR WARTS

Take as many small stones from a running stream as you have warts, put them tightly into a clean white bag, and throw them into the highway or street. Then wash each wart in strong vinegar seven successive mornings. Whosoever picks up the bag of stones will get a transfer of the warts.

TO HEAL BURNS

The witch repeats the following prayer while passing her hand three times over the burn:

"Three wise men came from the east,
One brought fire, two carried frost.
Out fire! In frost!
In the name of the Father, Son, and Holy Ghost."

CHARMS FOR TOOTHACHE

1 – Carry a dead person's tooth in the left waistcoat pocket.

2 – Bite a tooth from the jaw of a disinterred skull.

3 – "As Peter sat weeping on a stone our Saviour passed by and said, 'Peter, why weepest thou?' Peter said unto Him, 'I have got the toothache.' Our Saviour replied, 'Arise and be sound.'" And whosoever keeps this in memory or in writing will never suffer from toothache.

4 – Mix:
Two quarts of rat's broth.
One ounce of camphor.
One ounce essence of cloves
Dose – Take one teaspoonful three times a day.

ANOTHER TO CURE TOOTHACHE

Cut your toe and finger nails, take these parings, wrap in tissue paper, and insert the packet into a slit made in the bark of an ash tree before sunrise. You will never have toothache again as long as you live.

TO CURE THE COLIC

Mix equal quantities of elixir of toads and powdered Turkey rhubarb.
Dose – Half a teaspoonful fasting for three successive mornings.

TO CHARM A BRUISE

"Holy chicha! Holy chicha!
This bruise will get well by-and-bye.
Up sun high! Down moon low!
This bruise will be quite well very soon!00
In the Name of the Father, Son, and Holy Ghost.
Amen."

TO STAUNCH BLOOD

"As Christ was born in Bethlehem and baptized in the river Jordan, He said to the water, "Be still." So shall thy blood cease to flow. In the name of the Father, Son and Holy Ghost. – Amen."

ANOTHER REMEDY FOR STAUNCHING BLOOD

Take a fine full-grown toad; kill him, then take three bricks and keep in a very hot oven until they are red-hot. Take out one and place the toad upon it; when the brick is cold remove the toad; then take the other bricks and place the toad on them successively until he be reduced to powder. Then take the toad-ashes and sew them up carefully in a silk bag one-and-a-half inch square. When one is bleeding place this bag on the heart of the sufferer, and it will instantly stay the bleeding of the nose or any wound.

TO INSURE GOOD SIGHT

Fennel, rose, vervain, celandine and rue, do water make which will the sight renew.

CHARM FOR A THORN IN THE FLESH

"Our dear Lord Jesus Christ was pricked with thorns. His blood went back to Heaven again, His flesh neither cankered, rankled, nor festered, neither shall thine, M. or N. In the name of the Father, Son and Holy Ghost. – Amen, Amen, Amen."

THE HALF-CROWN CHARM FOR THE CURE OF KING'S EVIL

After morning service in the parish church, the nearest male relative, in the case of a woman; or in the case of a man, the nearest female relative, stations him or her self, on the right-hand side of the porch, holding his or her hat, into which young men (or women), between the ages of sixteen and twenty-one, drop a penny to the number of thirty. The pennies so collected are changed for a solver half-crown. The centre of this coin is cut out, and the outer ring is suspended as a charm to the neck of the afflicted person. The centre piece is reserved until the next funeral takes place, when it is dropped into the grave just before the coffin is lowered into it.

ANOTHER TO CURE KING'S EVIL

Bake a toad and when dried sufficiently to roll into powder, beat up in a stone mortar, mix with powdered vervain. Sew in a silken bag and wear round the neck.

TO CURE INFLAMMATION

Scour the inflamed part with strong brine, afterwards wash with plenty of soap, plenty too of hot water. Eat much raw beef for nine days.

AGAINST AGUE

For amulets against ague one must use chips of a gallows. These chips must be sewn into silken bags and worn near the heart.

TO CURE A SORE THROAT

Read the eighth Psalm seven times for three successive mornings over the patient.

TO CURE BLEEDING OF THE NOSE

Take one or two fine old toads, place them in a cold oven,

increase the heat until sufficiently fierce to cook the toads and reduce them to a brown crisp mass. Remove from the oven and beat them to powder in a stone mortar. Place the powder in a box and use as snuff!

ANOTHER CHARM TO STOP BLEEDING AT THE NOSE

Say nine times with great faith these words:
*"Blood abide in this vein as Christ abideth in the church,
And hide in thee as Christ hideth from himself."*

The bleeding will presently cease.

TO CURE DROPSY

Take several large fully-grown toads, place them in a vessel in which they can be burned without their ashes becoming mixed with any foreign matter. When reduced to ashes, pound them in a stone mortar. Place the ashes in a wide-mouthed jar, cork closely and keep in a dry place.

Dose. – One teaspoonful of ashes in milk to be taken at the growing of the moon for nine mornings.

TO CURE DIARRHOEA

Take a stale Good-Friday cross-bun and place it in a hot oven to dry. By grating when hard into powder, and when required, mixing it with cold water and taken as a medicine, it will cure diarrhoea.

*"When Good-Friday comes, an old woman runs
With one, or two-a-penny hot-cross-buns.
Whose virtue is, if you'll believe what's said,
They'll not grow mouldy like the common bread."*

TO CURE ITCHING

To cure itching in the palm of the hand –

*"Rub it on the eye,
'Twill go by-and-by;
Rub it on wood,
'Twill sure to come good."*

TO CURE SCIATICA OR BONESHAVE

Take a pale of clean river water, dipped from the down-flowing stream, a pair of shears, a large key, and a new table knife. Dip the knife into the pail of water, draw it back upwards, downwards and across the hip three times each way. Then dip the key into the water and proceed as before. Then dip the shears into water, shear the hip as though it were covered with wool. Return the water left in the bucket to the river and sing –

*"As this water goeth to zay,
So flow boneshave away."*

TO CURE BARNGUN, OR RINGWORM

Barngun is cured by blessing, and the outward application of clotted cream, thus: Take three locks of wool – one white, one grey, one black – dip them into a basin of clotted cream, and when thoroughly saturated, take each lock and rub in succession each infected spot on the skin. Hang the wool on sprigs of white thorn against the wind to dry. Repeat this process five, seven, or nine times, as the case may require. While lubricating the sores chant in monotone the following:

"There were three angels come from the west,
To cure Simon Fluke (or other) of the barngun,
White barngun, red barngu, black barngun,
Aching, sticking, pricking, barngun,
All sorts of barngun, barngun-būbee, ill will I prove 'e.
I stick thee up on these yer thorn, there thou shalt die,
And never come near 'n no more,
In the name of the Father, Son and Holy Ghost. – Amen"

A CURE FOR RHEUMATISM

An ancient Devonshire superstition is the potato-cure for rheumatism, which should be applied in this way.

Take a freshly dug early grown kidney potato, wash it free from soil, and ask a member of the opposite sex to yourself, to place it unobserved in a pocket of one of your garments. Having once worn the tuber you can change it yourself into another pocket at will, but it must be worn continuously, not intermittently, or its charm will be lost. It is believed that as the potato hardens the rheumatism will leave the system. A common practice among agricultural labourers, is to carry one in every waistcoat pocket until it looks like a small grey stone, and has become quite as hard.

A CHARM TO CURE WHOOPING COUGH

Bring an ass before the door of the house, into whose mouth thrust a slice of new bread, then pass the sick child three times over and under the animal's body, and the charm is completed.

TO CURE A FEVER

Write on parchment the following and bind it over the heart of the patient.

"In the name of St. Exuperus and St. Honorius, fall-fever, spring-fever, quartian, quintain, ago, super ago, consummatum est."

While fixing this charm to the patient, repeat three Paters and three Aves. The patient will recover after wearing the charm nine days.

❈ Charms for Protection ❈

TO FRUSTRATE THE POWER OF THE BLACK WITCH

Take a cast horse shoe, nail it over the front door, points upwards. While nailing it up chant in monotone the following:

*"So as the fire do melt the wax
And wind blows smoke away,
So in the presence of the Lord
The wicked shall decay,
The wicked shall decay. – Amen"*

THE ABRACADABRA CHARM.

The word "Abracadabra" written on parchment was given by an Exeter white witch, to a person who desired to possess a talisman against the dominion of the grey witch, pixies, evil spirits and the powers darkness! It cost a guinea, and was sewn up in a small black silk bag one inch square. This was hung round the neck and never removed.

```
A B R A C A D A B R A
 A B R A C A D A B R
  A B R A C A D A B
   A B R A C A D A
    A B R A C A D
     A B R A C A
      A B R A C
       A B R A
        A B R
         A B
          A
```

Should it by chance fall to the ground, all its properties for good would be lost and a new charm must be procured from the same white witch, or dire misfortune would overtake the owner. In "Reminiscences and Reflections," of an old West Country clergyman (the Rev. W. H Thornton, rector of North Bovey), the word "Abracadabra" occurs on page 44, in connection with a meeting of spiritualists, held in London in 1848.

CHARM FOR PROTECTION FROM ENEMIES

This talisman should be made from pure cast iron and engraven at the time of the new moon. Before suspending it round the neck fumigate it with the smoke of burnt Spirits of Mars (a mixture of red saunders, frankincense, and red pepper), or a ring of pure gold might be made, with the characters engraven on the inside. The size and form of this talisman is immaterial so long as the proper time for making it is observed and the prescribed incense is used before it is worn. In any form it will protect one from enemies, and counteract the power of the evil eye.

TO DISPEL VAPOURS AND DRIVE AWAY EVIL SPIRITS

St, John's Wort, or Devil's Flight, gathered on St John's Day or on a Friday, dried and placed in a closely-covered jar and hung in a window, will protect the house from thunderbolts, storms, fire, and evil spirits.

If the flowers and leaves are dried and ground into a powder and then placed in a silken bag and hung round the neck, the person will be successful in love, and be cured of the vapours and all mental afflictions. To insure perfect immunity from these ills, it is necessary to operate in July, on the evening of the full moon.

TO COUNTERACT THE EVIL OF SEEING BIRDS OF ILL OMEN

One should repeat seven times the following:

*"Clean birds by sevens, unclean birds by twos,
The dove in the heavens, is the bird which I choose."*

A CHARM WHICH PROTECTS FROM THIEVES AND ENEMIES

Say daily at sunrise:

*"In the power of God, I walk on my way
In the meekness of Christ, what thieves soe'er I meet
The Holy Ghost to-day shall me keep.
Whether I sit, stand, walk or sleep,*

*The shining of the sun
Also the brightness of his beams, shall me help.
The faith of Isaac to-day shall me lead;
The sufferings of Jacob to-day be my speed.
The devotion of the holy Lamb thieves shall let,
The strength of Jesus's passion them beset,
The dread of death hold thieves low,
The wisdom of Solomon cause their overthrow.
The sufferings of Job set them in hold,
The chastity of Daniel let what they would.
The speech of Isaac their speech shall spill,
The languishing faith of Jerom let them of their will.
The flaming fires of hell to hit them, I bequeath,
The deepness of the deep sea, their hearts to grieve
The help of Heaven cause thieves to stand.
He that made sun and moon bind them with his hand
So sure as St. Bartholomew bound the fiend,
With the hair of his beard.
With these three sacred names of God known and unknown.
Miser, Sue, Tetragrammaton, Christ Jesus! Amen."*

❈ Curses – to Cast & to Counter ❈

THE HERRING-BONE CHARM TO CAUSE DEATH

Sew into a garment which is worn next to the skin a long thin herring-bone. As the bone dries up, or withers, so will the person wearing it gradually pine away and die.

TO DESTROY THE POWER OF A WITCH

Take three small-necked stone jars: place in each the liver of a frog stuck full of new pins, and the heart of a toad stuck full of thorns from a holy thorn bush. Cork and seal each jar. Bury in three different churchyard paths seven inches from the surface and seven feet from the porch. While in the act of burying each jar repeat the Lord's prayer backwards. As the heart and livers decay so will the witch's power vanish. After performing this ceremony no witch can have any power over the operator.

Love Divination Charms

TO KNOW IF ONE'S PRESENT FIANCÉ WILL BE TRUE

Procure from a butcher a bladebone of a shoulder of lamb divested of all the meat. Borrow a penknife from an unmarried man, but do not say for what purpose it is required. Take a yard of white ribbon, and having tied it to the bone, hang it as high in the bedroom chimney as you can conveniently reach. On going to bed pierce the bone with the knife once, for nine successive nights, in a different place each night, repeat while doing so, the following:

*"Tiz not this bone I means to stick,
But my lover's heart I means to prick,
Wishing him neither rest nor sleep,
Till unto me he comes to speak."*

At the end of nine days your sweetheart will ask you to bind a wounded finger, or to attend to a cut which he will have met with during the time the charm was being used.

TO CAUSE A FUTURE SPOUSE TO APPEAR

Whoso wishes to see the spectre of a future husband can do so by performing the following rite. Retire to bed just before midnight, as quietly as possible. Remove the left garter, and tie it round the right stocking, while doing so repeat the following:

"This knot I knit, to know the thing I know not yet
That I may see, the man that shall my husband be,
How he goes, and what he wears,
And what he does all days and years."

During the night, the future "he" will appear dressed in his ordinary attire, carrying some badge of his trade or profession.

TO DISCOVER THE INITIALS OF YOUR FUTURE HUSBAND

On October 28th, the day dedicated to Saints Simeon and Jude, is the most propitious on which to use the following incantation for the discovery of the future one's initials. Take a fine round apple, peel it in one whole length. Take the paring in the right hand, stand in the centre of a large room, and while waving the paring gently round your head repeat:

"St. Simeon and St. Jude on you I intrude,
By this paring I hold to discover.

Without delay, tell me I pray,
The first letters of my own true lover."

Then drop the paring over the left shoulder and it will form the initial of your future husband's name; if it break up into small pieces you will die an old maid.

TO SEE ONE'S FUTURE HUSBAND BY CHARMING THE MOON

On seeing the new moon, make the sign of the cross three times in the air, and once on your forehead. Clasp both hands tightly together and hold them in a supplicating attitude, uplifted towards the moon. Then repeat:

"All hail, all hail, to thee,
All hail to thee, new moon.
I pray to thee, new moon,
Before thou growest old,
To reveal unto me,
Who my true love shall be!"

Before the moon is at full the supplicant will see her true love.

TO DISCOVER IF ONE WILL EVER MARRY

On Christmas eve go into the yard and tap smartly at the door of the hen-house. If a hen first cackles, you will never marry, but if a cock crows first then you will marry before the end of the coming year.

❄ Miscellaneous Charms ❄

TO SECURE LUCK AT GAMES OF CHANCE

Suspend by a silken cord around the neck, a section of the rope with which a person has been hanged.

TO RESTORE LOST MONEY

A white witch professed to be able to restore a lost sum of money by the following incantation.

"Flibberty, gibberty, flasky flum,
Calafac, tarada, lara, wagra wum.
Hooky, maroosky, whatever's the sum,
Heigho! Presto! Money come!
In the name of the Father, the Holy Ghost, and Son.
Amen! Amen!"

TO CHARM AWAY HOUSE FLIES

Gather and dry as much of the herb Fleabane as you can find. Each morning during the moths of June, July and August, burn a handful of the herb in the rooms. The smoke will drive the flies from the house.

TO PREVENT FLEAS FROM ENTERING A HOUSE

When you first hear the cuckoo in the Spring, take some of

the earth from the place on which your right foot is standing, and sprinkle it on the threshold of your front door; but speak of it to no one. Neither fleas, beetles, earwigs, or vermin of any sort will cross it.

TO BRING CREAM TO BUTTER

"Come, butter, come,
Come, butter, come,
Peter's waiting at the gate,
Waiting for a buttered cake.
Come, butter, come."

TO CURE ZWEEMY-HEADEDESS

Wash the head with plenty of old rum. The back and face with sour wine; wear flannel next to the skin, and carry a packet of salt in the left-hand pocket.

CHARM FOR OBTAINING LOVE AND FOR SUCCESS IN ALL UNDERTAKINGS

Whoever wears this charm, written on virgin parchment, and sewn up in a small round silken bag continuously over the heart, will obtain all the love he or she may desire, and will be successful in every undertaking.

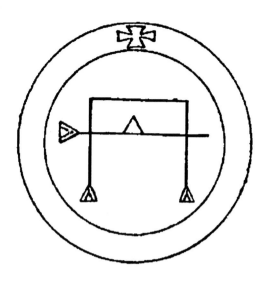

TO ASSIST CHILDREN IN TEETHING

Make a necklace of beads cut from the root of henbane and place round the child's neck.

TO BRING SPIRITS TO YOU

Anoint your eyes for three days with the combined juices of the herbs, dill, vervain, and St. John's-wort, and the spirits in the air will become visible to you.

A CHARM SUNG BY WITCHES WHILE GATHERING HERBS FOR MAGICAL PURPOSES

*"Hail to thee, holy herb,
Growing on the ground,*

All on Mount Calvary
First wast thou found.
Thou art good for many sores,
And healeth many a wound;
In the name of St. Jesu!
I take thee from the ground."

The muttering of this charm, while concocting drugs or simples, balsams or elixirs, contributes marvellously to their efficacy.

✠ SUPERSTITIONS ✠

❈ All Hallowe'en Superstitions ❈

I tell thee, there's not a pulse beats in the human frame that is not governed by the stars above us. The blood that fills our veins, in all its ebb and flow, is swayed by them as certainly as are the restless tides of the salt sea by the resplendent moon; and at thy birth thy mother's eye gazed not more steadfastly on thee, than did the star that rules thy fate, showering upon thy head an influence malignant or benign.

I think I cannot do better than describe what actually took place at an old farm house, in the eighties, in South Devon.

I was invited to spend a few days with a family, consisting of a farmer, his wife and seven grown-up sons and daughters. The farm was picturesquely situated on a south-western slope of the Haldon Hills, from whence extensive views of land and sea could be enjoyed.

Mary was the youngest and merriest of the family. She it was who acted as prime mover in all acts of fun, not that either of the others showed any reluctance to carry out her wildest suggestions. A brighter set of young folk it would be difficult to find, and it has seldom been my good fortune to meet their equals in high spirits and natural gentleness. Every one was thoroughly imbued with credulity in regard to omens and predictions.

Mary suggested that All Hallowe'en should be observed with due ceremony, as indeed it was. The amusements began with fortune-telling by cards, at which Maggie the eldest daughter was an adept. The fortunes were appraised as "not up to much," and as no one crossed Maggie's hand with a piece of silver, the cards were swept aside. Then Jack, otherwise the family clown, brought in dishes of apples and nuts, bags of hemp seed, torn paper, large basins of water, scraps of lead, a melting ladle, large combs, small hand mirrors, and a printed sheet of capital letters, all of which were to be used as love-charms.

Just as the clock began to strike eleven, a move was made towards the fireplace, where from the bars of the grate Jack had already swept every vestige of ashes. Simultaneously each girl laid a big hazel nut on the lowest bar of the grate, and sat silently watching the result. I noticed that perfect silence was religiously observed during each ceremony. She, whose nut first blazed, would be the first to marry. She, whose nut first cracked, would be jilted. She, whose nut first jumped, would very soon start on a journey, but would never marry. She, whose nut smouldered, would have sickness, disappointment in love, and perhaps die young.

After this, one of the girls took an apple, a comb, and a mirror, and retired to the brightest corner of the room, where she began to comb out her long tresses with her left hand and held an apple in the right, which she slowly ate. Her future husband was expected to look over her shoulder, revealing his face to her in the mirror. He did not, however, satisfy our curiosity by putting in an appearance.

Then one took a handful of torn paper and scattered it on the surface of a big basin of water, and after stirring vigorously, awaited developments. The number of pieces of paper which fell to the bottom indicated the number of years which would intervene before the operator's marriage. In this case twenty-one fell, and as Jenny was now twenty-eight, Jack thought there was small chance for her to have an establishment of her own at forty-nine, so she had better resign herself to her fate, and be content to become the unappropriated blessing of the family, for, said he, "how could you, Jenny, at that advanced age, dare to don white satin and orange blossoms? No, my dear, your future is sealed."

Then everybody insisted on Jack trying his luck, which he essayed to do by melting a few scraps of lead in the ladle and pouring it red hot into one of the basins of cold water. The letters formed, or the nearest approach to letters, at the bottom of the basin were supposed to be the initials of the future "she." The closest resemblance to letters which we could discover was an I, and an L. The question which now arose amid merry peals of laughter was to whom the initials I.L. could belong. Many names were mentioned and negatived as soon as suggested, Jack looking rather bashful, when from Jenny came the query – "Does not I stand for Ida, and L for Lang? Ida Lang is a very pretty name and is owned by a very sweet girl." Jack gave Jenny a look which could easily be interpreted "I owe you one for that, Jenny" – "Oh! Oh! Jack" replied Jenny, "we are hoping that Ida Lang will not be an unappropriated blessing. She shall have my white satin and all the orange blossoms." There was a good deal more of this sort of chaff, but no offence was taken by the good-natured Jack, and things swung along amicably.

Next came Tom to try his hap with a pair of scissors. Tom in silence separated the capital letters, each falling into the basin of water without being touched by the hand. When all were free they were stirred and left to settle. The initials of the future one, were supposed to float on the water. Alas! Poor Tom! In his case fifteen letters presented themselves. Here again was food for fun and conjecture. Many suggestions were made. Tom, perhaps was going to be a Mormon, or perhaps he was going abroad and set up a harem, and all sorts of other absurd theories. Mary at last came to the rescue, "Oh, I know," said she, "take G and M out and there you have Gertrude Morley, then tack all the rest on to the end of the name, and there you have certain degrees won by Gertrude at the 'Varsity. Gertrude is a Newnham student. Last autumn in the long vacation there was a young woman of that strain dodging across the hills, and on one occasion when she saw our Tom cantering towards her, her bike became fractious instanter, and poor innocent Tom had to dismount, tie Highflyer to a gatepost and assist the distressed biker. Of course, Tom couldn't help himself and had to lead Highflyer up the hill and push the bike too." Alas poor Tom! Then turning to her mother she explained that Tom was about to present her with a new daughter in the form of a Newnham girl so vastly clever, that she used up all the alphabet to shew how clever she was and the heaps of degrees she took, &c., &c. "I say, Tom, do you think Gertrude Morley, B.A., M.D., M.G.L.Q.R., will like taking my place in the house work, and be able to cry chuggie, chuggie, chuggie, every morning to the dear little piggy-wiggies; perhapse though, instead of giving them barley-meal and milk, she'll sit them all in a row, in the bottom of the trough, and teach 'em Latin and Greek don't-cher-know; eh, Tom dear?"

Heedless of this affectionate raillery, everything drifted along smoothly, and four dishes of water were brought in and placed severally in three corners of the room, and the fourth, emptied of its contents, was placed in the fourth corner. Then four blind-folded operators were led into the room and placed back to back in its centre, the lights having been previously extinguished. Then all four fell on their knees and each crept at discretion to any, or all to the same, corner. The empty dish portended celibacy or poverty. The dish of clean water, that the future one would never before have married. The dish of dirty water, that the future spouse would be a widow or widower. The dish of water with pebbles at the bottom, riches and honour.

Now the crucial movement was at hand. Each girl took possession of a big handful of hempseed. The front door was thrown wide open and securely fastened back to prevent the possibility of its being accidentally closed. The girls stood without. As the clock gave the first stroke of twelve off they started each in a different direction across the lawn, shouting:

"Hempseed I sow,
Hempseed I throw,
He that's my true-love,
Come after me and mow!"

The spirits of the future ones were expected to be beyond the shrubs ready to rush after the sowers, and unhappy would have been the maiden, who could not get over the threshold before the scythe of the future reaper caught her. All the girls reached the hall unharmed: little Mary, looking a bit scared, she said, as she wound her arms around me: "Oh, wasn't I just about startled? Indeed I was, for I thought I saw Dick Harvey right in front of me as I turned to come back, holding a bright new sickle over his head." I felt the child tremble, and then I enquired, "Who is Dick Harvey?" "Oh, nobody in particular, don't tell." Of course I have not told till now.

After supper we retired for the night. The next morning the girls told me, that sometimes they placed tiny scraps of bridecake, wrapped in tissue paper, under their pillows at night, hoping they would dream of "him:" at other times made a "dumb cake," and gave me a recipe for making one, which I append. Jenny told me too, that one evening when visiting friends at Paignton, one of the party saw for the first time the new moon: she called all the young folk out on the balcony requesting each to bring a small hand-mirror, to turn their back to the moon, and holding up the mirrors to catch the reflection of the moon. As many reflections as were cast on the glass, so many years would pass before the marriage of the holder took place. One charming girl of the party told me: "I had three moons. Fancy that, my dear, and you know how very old I am now, and have three years of weary waiting yet."

That delightful family is broken up. The parents are both dead, and the children are scattered to the ends of the earth. Not one is left in England. Each member has carried the old songs, the old dialect, and the old folk-lore of the old country, into new homes, in new countries, and there in time a new generation will spring up, who will be taught the traditions of the past; and perhaps the incidents of that happy All Hallowe'en, spent amidst the uplands of dear old Devon, will form one of the pleasantest narrations.

Poor Dick Harvey never came to claim little Mary, for, very soon after that happy evening, news came of a great storm, and Dick, who was first officer of the ss. Petrel, was lost with all hands in mid Atlantic.

Everywhere throughout the length and breadth of Great Britain, the festive and fortune-telling practices of this evening are observed in almost identical fashion. Gray, in The Spell, tells us that –

"Two hazel-nuts I threw into the fire,
And to each nut I gave a sweetheart's name.
This, with the loudest bounce, me sore amazed,
That, in a flame of brightest colour blazed:
As blazed the nut so may thy passion grow,
For 'twas thy nut that did so brightly glow."

Then we have in Nut burning on All Halloweve, by Charles Graydon, the following –

"These glowing nuts are emblems true,
Of what in human life we view;
The ill-matched couple fret and fume,
And thus in strife themselves consume;
Or from each other wildly start,
And with a noise for ever part.
But see the happy, happy pair,
Of genuine love and truth sincere
With mutual fondness while they burn,
Still to each other kindly turn;
And as the vital sparks decay,
Together gently sink away:
Till life's fierce ordeal being past,
Their mingled ashes rest at last."

Burns, too, contributes a long poem on "Halloween," which gives us an insight into the manners and traditions of the peasantry in the West of Scotland in his time.

"The old goodwife's well hoarded nuts
Are round and round divided:
And many lads' and lasses' fates
Are there that night decided:
Some kindled, couthie, side by side
And burn together trimly;
Some start away with saucy pride
And jump out o'er the chimney
Full high that night."

RECIPE FOR MAKING A DUMB CAKE

In the preparation of a dumb cake, if perfection be desired, it is imperative to observe strict silence, and to follow these instructions closely.

Let any number of unmarried ladies each take a handful of wheaten flour, and place it on a sheet of white paper, then sprinkle it with as much salt as can be held between finger and thumb; then one must put as much clear spring-water as will make it into dough, which being done, each of the party must roll it up, and spread it thin and broad, and each maid must, at some distance apart, make the first letters of their christian and surname with a large new pin, towards the end of the cake; if more christian-names than one, the first letter of each one must be made. Then set the cake before the fire, then each girl must sit down in a chair, as far from the fire as the room will admit, not speaking a word all the time. This must be done between eleven and twelve o'clock at night. Each person in rotation must turn the cake once, and five minuets after midnight the husband of her who is to be wed first will appear and lay his hand upon that part of the cake bearing her initials. – from the Norwood Gipsy Fortune-teller.

If the cake be eaten, strict silence must be observed from the moment a slice is cut. The person walks backwards from the room, up the stairs, and after undressing goes into bed, still backwards. Stumbling and giggling are inadmissible. It is presumed that happy dreams of "the loved one" will occupy the hours of slumber.

Omens and Death Tokens

Addison says, "We suffer as much from trifling accidents as from real evils. I have known the shooting of a star spoil a night's rest, and have seen a man in love grow pale and lose his appetite upon the plucking of a merrythought. A screech-owl at midnight has alarmed a family more than a band of robbers; nay, the voice of a cricket has struck more terror than the roaring of a lion. There is nothing so inconsiderable which may not appear dreadful to an imagination that is filled with omens and prognostications. A rusty nail or a crooked pin shoot up into prodigies."

Belief in omens is not confined to the simple and uneducated, but permeate every social grade. Omens are said to be the "poetry of history." Mary de Medici saw, in a dream, the brilliants of her crown change into pearls – symbols of tears and mourning. The Stuart monarchs held that their sorrows and misfortunes were foretokened. The learned Earl of Roscommon and Dr. Johnson were believers in spectres and supernatural agencies. The mountaineer makes the natural phenomena which daily present themselves to him foretokens of weal or woe. Dwellers in low-lying countries, too, find signs in their surroundings to distress and disturb their piece of mind. Each is continually inviting bugbears to harass and worry him.

There is a strong belief that the robin, raven, magpie, owl, and a nameless white bird, by the manner of their flight, and other peculiarities of action, foretell the approaching dissolution of some member of the household which they visit. A robin sitting near a window, uttering a plaintive weep,- weep,- weep,- presages sickness and death; if he flies into an occupied bedroom, then, death is near at hand. A remarkable instance of credulity in robin-lore came to my notice in 1891. the following was told to me by an educated lady, whose temperament is in no way morbid or hysterical; but is in herself bright, cheerful, and religious. The sight of a robin carries her memory back to some of the saddest days of her life. Here is her story:-

"in 1848 I was staying with my grandparents at Ashburton, in Devonshire. My grandmother, having a severe cold, went early to bed, and the weather being oppressively hot, the window was left open. Presently a robin, dishevelled and melancholy, flew into the room and perched on the towel-rail. No amount of persuasion could dislodge him, and at last all efforts to eject him were abandoned. He continued his sad weep,- weep,- weep,- for at least an hour, when he quietly flew out of the window. That night grannie died. Again, in 1851, a robin, just as unhappy and forlorn as the former one, flew into my father's bedroom, exhibiting every sign of dejection. Nor would he be easily driven off, but sought the tester of the bed, where he continued his weep,- weep,- weep. That night my father died. Again, in the autumn of 1884, while on a visit to Dawlish with my husband and children, we often took our books and work into the garden. One evening, as usual, we were in the summer-house, the children playing noisily, when a robin flew into their midst, and hopped on the table, finally perching himself on the handle of my work-basket. A more pitiable dejected little birdie could not be imagined, his feathers were ruffled and touselled, and both wings drooped to his feet. There he sat, uttering his dolorous weep,- weep, weep,- for several minuets; when we rose to go into the house he followed, sometimes fluttering along before us in the path, at others flitting from bush to bush close at our side. Even after we had closed the window we heard him on the shrubs outside, still pathetically uttering his doleful weep,- weep,- weep. The next morning my dear husband, who had gone along the Strand for a stroll while I dressed the children for a walk, dropped suddenly dead, and was brought home within a quarter of an hour after leaving the house. Can you wonder at my having dread of a visit from a robin after these pitiful experiences?"

THE DEATH-WATCH

One often hears issuing from the rafters and wood-work of old houses sounds resembling the ticking of a watch. These clickings are produced by a small insect known as the "Death-Watch." By nervous persons they are considered omens of death.

A wood-worm
That lies in old wood, like a hare in her form,
With teeth or with claws it will bite, or will scratch;
And chambermaids christen this worm a death-watch
Because like a watch it always cries click;
Then woe be to those in the house that be sick,

For, sure as a gun, they will give up the ghost.
If the maggot cries click when it scratches the post
But a kettle of scalding hot water ejected,
Infallibly cures the timber affected.
The omen is broken, the danger is over;
The maggot will die, the sick will recover.

OTHER DEATH TOKENS

If a corpse retains heat and flexibility it is said that others of the same family will die before the year is out.

If a sheet or tablecloth is returned from the laundry with a square fold in the centre, so it is said to portend the death of the master or mistress of the house.

If letters cross in the post it is a sign of death.

Marriage Ceremony Superstitions

There are many superstitious customs attached to the marriage ceremony, some of which are supposed to endow the pair with blessings and an abundant share of the good things of life, while others bring only misfortune and disquietude.

Witches and pixies alas, are workers of evil, and beset the path of the bride and bridegroom to and from the church, plying their wicked tricks to the detriment of the happy pair. The days of the week, too, on which the ceremony is performed, influence their future, as the following lines testify:

Monday for wealth,
Tuesday for health,
Wednesday is the best day of all,
Thursday for crosses,
Friday for losses,
Saturday no luck at all.

Sunday is an exceptionally fortunate day upon which to enter the holy state. One often hears:

"Happy is the bride that the sun shines upon."

Among the customs bringing good luck to the pair, are pelting them with rice as they leave the church after the ceremony, and throwing old slippers at them, too, as they leave the house for the honeymoon.

Happiness can be insured by observing certain practices which have been in vogue for many centuries, as for example: it is necessary to carry sprigs of rue and rosemary and a few cloves of garlic in the pocket, to enhance the felicity of the pair. The bride also should carry a small packet of bread and cheese in her pocket to give to the first woman or girl she meets after leaving the church. Dire calamities will overtake the couple if either of these cherished practices are omitted, though the perfume of garlic and rue added to the wedding bouquets seems incongruous.

Now follow the unfortunate omens and events attached to this momentous occasion. Should a raven hover over their path, a cat, dog, or hare pass between them, or should they encounter a toad, frog, or other reptile, then terrible misfortunes will follow them for all time. These creatures are supposed to be the embodiment of pixies, witches, and every species of evil spirit. Even his satanic majesty does not object to assume the form of an animal, to enable him to work certain ill on their future lives, and to assist in contributing his share to their distress.

In Devon, when a wife is of stronger will than her husband, the people say, "Aw ess, the grey mare in thickee 'ouze is the better 'oss," and ascribe her masterfulness to her having visited and drank of the water of the well of St. Keyne, in Cornwall.

Divination by the Bible

A person wishing to know whether success or failure is to attend his future, should open the Bible at the forty-ninth chapter of Genesis, begin with the third verse and end with the twenty-seventh; the verse he first chooses will be typical of his future fate, character, and success in life.

Another method practiced by country folk on almost every occasion, is to open the Bible at random, and the words which first present themselves decides the future lot of the enquirer.

In Devonshire, many persons when they have lost anything, and suspect it to have been stolen, take the front door key of their dwelling, and, in order to find out the thief, tie this key to the Bible, placing it very carefully on the eighteenth verse of the fiftieth Psalm. ("When thou sawest a thief, then thou consentedst with him, and hast been partaker with adulterers.") Two persons must then hold the book by the bow of the key, and first repeat the name of the suspected thief, and then the verse from the Psalm. If the Bible moves, the suspected person is considered guilty; if it does not move, innocent.

❋ Clover & Ash-Leaf Superstition ❋

An even leaved ash and a four leaved clover
Are certain to bring to me my true love
Before the day is over.

An even leaved ash and a four leaved clover are beneficent attractors of the opposite sex, for if one finds an even leaved ash and holds it flat between both hands, and repeats softly,

"With this even leaved ash between my hands
the first I meet will be my dear man."

Then placing it in the palm of the gloved right hand, say,

"This placed in my glove
Will bring my own true love."

Then remove it to the bosom and whisper,

"This even leaved ash in my bosom
Will give me, in the first man I meet
My true husband."

About Salt

Salt, in country districts, is held as a sacred article, and the vessel used to contain it is considered hallowed and looked upon as a valuable possession. Dire calamities follow on spilling salt, and a charm is used to counteract the dread consequences. An old nurse once told me that if a plate of salt be placed on the breast of a corpse, it would help the dead to rest peacefully, as it kept evil spirits from tormenting the soul on its journey through the dark valley.

An old Devonshire friend has sent me the following lines, which he is in the habit of repeating when small matters go wrong in the household. I believe they were written by the poet Gay, from whom he must have learnt them when a child.
Alas, you know the cause too well!
The salt is spilt: to me it fell;
Then, to contribute to my loss,
My knife and fork were laid across:
On Friday, too, the day I dread.
Would I were safe at home in bed!
Last night (I vow to heaven 'tis true)
Bounce from the fire a coffin flew.
Next post some fatal news shall tell
God send my absent friends are well!

Oneiromancy

Oneiromancy is the art of interpreting dreams. This kind of divination is still in use among the masses, and has been practiced from the most remote ages. In rural districts there are to be found ancient dames whose interpretations of dreams are looked upon with reverence, and are a source of revenue to the old women.

At breakfast it is not uncommon for members of a family to narrate their dreams, and seek the elucidation thereof.

"A dream in an ill-arranged action of the thinking faculties during a state of partial sleep, and is but a momentary impression, perfectly natural in its operation; the state of mind causes it being produced by temporary functional derangement."

If I dream of water pure,
Before the coming morn,
'Tis a sign I shall be poor,
and unto wealth not born.
If I dream of tasting beer,
Middling then will be my cheer –
Chequered with the good and bad,
Sometimes joyful, sometimes sad;
But should I dream of drinking wine,
Wealth and pleasure will be mine.
The stronger the drink, the better the cheer,
Dreams of my destiny appear.

The belief that dreams are indicative or symbolical of coming events is very common among the masses. Some persons look upon dreams as absolutely true mediums of revealing the secrets of futurity. The following examples shew "the stuff which dreams are made of."

Ass
To dream one sees an ass labouring under a heavy burden, indicates that one will by diligent application to business amass a fortune.

Absent Ones
To dream of these ill, or in trouble, shows they are in danger; if well, it is a sign they are prosperous.

Angels
A happy dream, showing peace at home, and a good understanding with your friends.

Baby
If you dream of holding a baby in your arms it signifies trouble.

Bells
If you hear them ring it is a good sign, foretelling luck in business and a speedy marriage.

Bees
That you see a swarm of bees signifies you will be wise and highly respected. If they disturb or sting you, you will lose friends, and your sweetheart will abandon you.

Carriage
If you dream that you are shut up in a carriage and cannot get out, it shows that your false friends are scandalizing you; and you will suffer much at their hands.

Cats
Dreaming of cats shews that your female friends are

treacherous.

Cards
If you dream you are playing cards it signifies that you will shortly be married.

Dancing
This is fortunate. You will gain riches, honour, and many friends. Your life will be long, happy, and prosperous.

The Dead
To dream of the dead brings news of the living.

Ducks
To see them in a pond swimming about is an omen of good luck.

Eggs
That you are eating eggs shews that you will be delivered from great tribulation. That you break them when raw, shows loss of friends and fortune.

Empty Vessels
Shew that your life will be one of toil and privation.

Eating
Portends sickness and death.

Fish
To dream of fish shows that you will have an abundance of wealth and good things. Also that you will be successful in love.

Fire
To dream of fire shews that you will have hasty news.

Flowers
Always a good dream; is a sure sign of joy, success and prosperity.

Garden
To dream of being in a beautiful garden shews you will be rich and prosperous in love.

Glass
Broken glass foretells quarrels and family strife.

Gold
To dream of gold portends riches.

Hares
To dream of these implies great trouble in pecuniary matters and sickness.

Horses
Shews that your life will be long and happy. If kicked by a horse you will have a long and sever illness, and heavy misfortune.

Ivy
A sign that your friendships are true.

Inn
To dream that you are staying at an inn is a most favourable one. It shews that you will inherit a large fortune, be successful in all your undertakings, and will enjoy much happiness.

Jackdaw
Beware of danger and evil disposed persons.

Journey
If you are about to take one in your dream, you will meet with reverse of fortune.

Knives
Are always omens of some evil about to happen.

Kiss
To dream that some one is kissing you, is a sure sign that you are being deceived. To dream that you are kissing some one whom you love is a sign that your love is not reciprocated.

Larks
To dream of these birds is a good sign, as it denotes that you will overcome all difficulties that may come in your way, and you will speedily rise to a good position.

Lightening
Without thunder is one of the very luckiest dreams. To lovers it means happiness; to farmers, good crops, and to sailors, prosperous voyages.

Mad Dogs
In dreams these are omens of success.

Magpies
That you will soon be married.

Nightingales

Nightingales singing are indicative of bright days coming and a release from all troubles and anxieties.

Nuts
Indicate the receipt of money.

Oats
Are lucky omens of success

Onions
If you dream you are eating them you will find much money.

Pall
One over a coffin is prophetic of a wedding dress.

Parcel
If you carry one you should receive a foreign letter.

Quarrels
If you dream of them it is a sign that you will soon be very profitably engaged in a business matter.

Rain
Is an omen of misfortune.

Rats
Prophesy enemies near at hand.

Teeth
To dream of, are the most unlucky of all things. If they fall out it signifies much sickness, if they all drop from the gums, death.

Ships
Sailing in clear water are favourable omens, but if the water be murky, most unfavourable.

Silver Coins
Picking them up, unless there be gold with them, is significant of impecuniosity.

Ugliness
If you see yourself reflected as very ugly it is an omen of success.

Umbrellas
If you lose them it signifies losses in business.

Valentine
Dreaming of receiving one is a bad sign, illness and trouble will soon be upon you.

Violin
If you are playing one in your dream, it denotes speedy marriage; unless a string breaks, then you will not marry at all.

Water
Dreaming of water, if it be clear will bring good news, if dirty, bad news is at hand.

Wedding
One dreamed of signifies a funeral.

Yachting
In clear water on a sunny day is prophetic of very great happiness.

Yew Trees
You will hear of the death of an aged person in whom you have a vested interest.

In Mackay's *Popular Delusions, 1869,* occurs the following passage, which seems too good too omit.

"Dreams, say all the wiseacres, are to be interpreted by contraries. Thus, if you dream of filth, you will acquire something valuable; if of gold and silver, you run the risk of being without either; if of many friends, you will be persecuted by many enemies. The rule does not, however, hold good in all cases. It is fortunate to dream of little pigs, but unfortunate to dream of big bullocks. If you dream of fire you will have nasty news from a far country; if of vermin, you will have sickness in your family; if of serpents, your friends will become your bitterest enemies; if you are wallowing up to your neck in mud and mire, you will be most fortunate in all your undertakings. Clear water is a sign of grief; and great troubles, distress and perplexity are predicted if you dream you are standing naked in the public streets and know not where to turn for a garment to shield you from the gaze of the multitude."

To dream of walking in a field,
Where new-born roses odours yield;
If any of them you do pluck,
It shews in love much happy luck.
To dream of mountains, hills, or rocks,
Does signify flouts, scoffs, and mocks;
Their pains in passing ever shew
That she whom you love, loves not you.
Dreams of joy and pleasant jests,

*Dancing, merriment, and feasts,
Or any dream of recreation
Signifies love's declaration.
Dreams full f horror and confusion
Ending merrily in conclusion,
Shews storms of love are overblown,
And after sorrow joy shall come.*

From Forty's Norwood Gipsy's Fortune-teller.

ST. MARK'S EVE

Repair to the nearest churchyard as the clock strikes twelve, and take from a grave on the south side of the church three tufts of grass, and on going to bed place them under your pillow, repeating earnestly three several times,

*"The eve of St. Mark by prediction is blest,
Set therefore my hopes and my fears all to the rest:
Let me know my fate, whether weal or woe;
Whether my rank's to be high or low;
Whether to live single or to be a bride,
And the destiny my star doth provide."*

Should you have no dream that night, you will be single and miserable all your life. If you dream of thunder and lightening, your life will be one of great difficulty and sorrow.

ST. JOHN'S EVE

Make a new pincushion of the very best black silk velvet

(none other will do), and on one side stick your name in the very smallest pins you can buy; on the other side make a cross with some large pins, and surround it with a circle. Put this into your left-foot stocking when you take it off at nigh, and hang it up at the foot of the bed. All your future life will pass before you in a dream. – Mackay's *Popular Delusions*.

The Mistletoe Curse

Mistletoe, a parasite chiefly found on oak and apple trees, was held in great esteem by the Druids, who affirmed that miraculous cures were effected by its means. They ascribed to it a divine origin, and bestowed upon it the name "Curer-of-all-ills."

The trees on which it grew, and the birds visiting their branches, were considered sacred, and were thought to be messengers of the gods. When mistletoe was required for the performance of their sacred offices, great ceremony was observed in separating it from the limbs on which it grew; the priests using a golden sickle for the purpose.

Devonions believe that their county was cursed by these ancient religious fathers, and the mistletoe forbidden by them to grow in it. Why this curse was laid on Devon there is no record to show. A gentleman possessed an orchard, one half of which is in Devon, and the other in Somersetshire, the division of the counties being marked by a deep ditch. On the Devon side the apple-trees are free, while on the Somerset side this parasite grows in abundance. He has tried in vain to cultivate it on trees in the banned county.

❄ Legend of the Glastonbury ❄ Thorn

When Joseph of Arimathea came to England he visited Glastonbury, so the legend says, and being wearied with the long climb up the hill, halted and leaned on his stout blackthorn staff. The stick sank into the soft mud on the wayside, took root, grew, and bloomed on Old Christmas Eve. There it stands to this day and always repeats the operation each successive year. There is also a sacred spring at its roots, in which thousands of persons came to bathe on Old Christmas Eve, A.D. 1751.

This marvellous thorn has a rival in the grounds of Clooneaven House, at Lynmouth, N. Devon, where the little bush bursts into vigorous bloom for a few hours at Christmastide. Very soon its flowers fade and the plant assumes its normal condition until the following spring, when it puts on its pretty green dress like the rest of its species.

❄ The Chagford Pixies ❄

As a gentleman, late at night, was driving across the moor to Chagford, a village in mid-Devon, he was startled by the merry tinkle of tiny bells. Lights appeared in the meadows close at hand as of thousands of glow-worms shedding their luminous rays on every leaflet, while an innumerable company of small people tripped joyously to the supportive music. Every movement of this assemblage of fairies was distinctly seen by him. He reined in his horse, and watched for a considerable time their merry antics. He sat motionless, the better t catch the spirit of the sportive scene. The sward was crowded with myriads of sprites, some waving garlands of tiny wild flowers, roses and blue bells, others joining in the dance, while not a few bestrode the slender stalks of tall grasses, which scarcely bent beneath their feathery weight. All went merrily till the shrill crow of chanticleer rang out on the midnight air, when suddenly darkness fell and the gorgeous scene with its fantastically attired crowd vanished from the wayfarer's sight.

The villagers assert that on peaceful nights they often hear the echoes of delightful music and the tripping patter of tine feet issuing from the meadows and hill sides.

"By wells and rills, in meadows green
We nightly dance our heyday guise,
And to our fairy king and queen
We chant our moonlight minstrelsies,
When larks 'gin sing'
Away we fling,
And babes new-born steal as we go;
And elf in bed,
We leave instead,
And wend us laughing, ho! ho! ho!"

❈ The Ghost of the Black-Dog ❈

A man having to walk from Princetown to Plymouth took the road which crosses Roborough Down. He started at four o'clock from the Duchy Hotel, and as he walked at a good swinging pace, hoped to cover the sixteen miles in about three hours and a half. It was a lovely evening in December, cold and frosty, the stars and a bright moon giving enough light to enable him to see the roadway distinctly zigzagged across the moor. Not a friendly pony or a quiet Neddy crossed his path as he strode merrily onward whistling as he went. After a while the desolation of the scene seemed to strike him, and he felt terribly alone among the boulders and huge masses of gorse which hemmed him in. On, on he pressed, till he came to a village where a wayside inn tempted him to rest awhile and have just one nip of something "short" to keep his spirits up.

Passing the reservoir beds, he came out on an open piece of road, with a pine copse on his right. Just then he fancied he heard the pit-pat of feet gaining upon him. Thinking it was a pedestrian bound for Plymouth, he turned to accost his fellow traveller, but there was no one visible, nor were any footfalls then audible. Immediately on resuming his walk, pit-pat, pit-pat, fell the echoes of feet again. And suddenly there appeared close to his right side an enormous dog, neither mastiff or bloodhound, but what seemed to him to be a Newfoundland of immense size. Dogs were always fond of him, and he of them, so he took no heed of this (to him) lovely canine specimen. Presently he spoke to him. "Well, doggie, what a beauty you are: how far are you going?" at the same time lifting his hand to pat him. Great was the man's astonishment to find no resisting substance, though the form was certainly there, for his hand passed right through the seeming body of the animal. "Hulloh! what's this?" said the bewildered traveller. As he spoke the great glassy eyes gazed at him; then the beast yawned, and from his throat issued a stream of sulphurous breath. Well, thought the man, I an in for it now! I'll trudge on as fast as legs can carry me, without letting this queer customer think I am afraid of him. With heart beating madly, and feet actually flying over the stony way, he hurried down the hill, the dog never for a moment leaving him, or slackening his speed. They soon reached a crossway, not far from the fortifications. When suddenly the man was startled by a loud report, followed by a blinding flash, as of lightening, which struck him senseless to the ground. At daybreak, he was found by the driver of the mail-cart, lying in a ditch at the roadside in an unconscious state. Tradition says, that a foul murder was many years ago committed at this spot, and the victim's dog is doomed to traverse this road and kill every man he encounters, until the perpetrator of the deed has perished by his instrumentality.

There are similar legends of the doings of the Black Dog throughout the country, and many wayside public houses have "The Black Dog" for a sign.

Superstitions Attached to Church Bells

In ancient times church bells were anointed with holy oil, exorcised, and blessed by the bishop, from a belief that when these ceremonies had been performed, they had the power to drive the devil out of the air, to calm tempests, protect from lightening, and keep away the plague.

The passing bell was anciently rung to bespeak the prayers of all Christian people for a soul just departing, and to drive away the evil spirit who stood at the bed's foot to hinder its passage to the otherworld.

"Men's death I tell by doleful knell,
Lightening and thunder I break asunder,
The winds so fierce I do disperse,
Men's cruel rage I do assuage."

A very frequent inscription on church bells in the fifteenth century, was voce mea viva depells cunta novicea.

This is a proof of the belief that demons were frightened away by the sound of bells. In a Cornish belfry the following rhyme is found suspended against the wall.

"Therefore I'd have you not to vapour,
Nor blame the lads that use the clapper,
Y which are scared the fiends of hell,
And all by virtue of a bell."

The Seventh Son

Many persons believe that a seventh son can cure diseases, but that a seventh son of a seventh son, and no female child born between, can cure the king's Evil.

Sunday

In the West of England, Sunday is reckoned to be the day for leaving off any article of clothing, as then those who so divest themselves will have the prayers of every congregation on their behalf, and are sure not to catch a cold.

It has also been remarked that rooks never attempt to build their nests on Sunday, even though there are but a few twigs necessary to complete them.

Some persons object to cut their nails, or turn a feather bed on Sunday.

✣ THINGS LUCKY ✣ & UNLUCKY

For every ill beneath the sun
There is some remedy, or none.
Should there be one, resolve to find it,
If not, submit; and never mind it.

It is difficult to define accurately the word 'unlucky' as understood by people in general. It conveys to their minds an indistinct supernatural and distressful affliction, of an awful character, and for a long time a troubled restlessness and fear of approaching evil embitters every moment of their lives, until the haunting dread wears itself out.

❋ It is Lucky… ❋

To stumble on ascending stairs, steps or ladders: it indicates a speedy marriage.

To find a cast horse-shoe.

To see the new moon over the right shoulder if one is out of doors.

To see a pin and pick it up will bring the very best of luck.

To break a piece of pottery on Good Friday.
To carry crooked coins in the pocket.

To receive the right hand of the bishop on one's head at confirmation.

To sow all kinds of garden seeds on Good Friday. Beans and peas sown on this day yield better crops.

To plant all kinds of ornamental shrubs on Good Friday.

To see a company of fairies dancing in the adit of a mine, as it indicates the presence of valuable loads.

To pay money on the first of January, as it insures the blessing of ready cash for all payments throughout the year.

To spit over the right shoulder when one meets a grey horse.

To meet a flock of sheep on the highway when on a journey.

To throw a pinch of salt into the mash when brewing, to kep the witches out.

To rest bars of iron on vessels containing beer in summer. They prevent "souring of the liquor" in thundery weather.

To have crickets in the house.

To see a star on the wick of a candle.

*"There's a star in the candle to-night,
One bright little spot shining clear,
To make our heavy hearts light,
By shewing that a letter is near."*

To carry a badger's tooth in the waistcoat pocket: it brings luck at cards.

To have white specks on one's finger nails shews that happiness is in store. These specks are sometimes called "gifts."

*"A gift on the thumb is sure to come,
A gift on the finger is sure to linger."*

Or they may be thus enumerated:

*"A gift, a friend, a foe,
A lover to come, a journey to go."*

To be born on Sunday; because you can see spirits, and tame the dragon who watches over hidden treasure.

To bite a baby's nails before it is a year old instead of cutting them, as it ensures its honesty through life.

To put the left stocking on first.

To put the right foot first, because it ensures success.

To fell trees at the wane of the moon, and when the wind is

in the North.

To be the seventh son of a seventh son, for he can, by passing his hand over the glands of the neck of a person suffering from King's Evil, cure the disease.

On first hearing the cuckoo in spring one should run in a circle three times with the sun, to ensure good luck for the rest of the year. If one hears the cuckoo to the right it portends good fortune, but to hear his voice on the left is a sure sign of impending misfortune. On hearing the cuckoo's note in April run as fast as possible to the nearest gate, and sit on the top bar to drive away the spirits of laziness. Who neglects to do this will be weak for a year, and have no inclination to work until the ensuing spring when the harbinger of spring again returns.

To possess a rope by which a person has been hanged ensures god luck.

On opening a new business, or entering upon any new commercial enterprise, the first money taken should be turned over from hand to hand and spat upon, to insure good luck in all future dealing.

❄ It is Unlucky… ❄

To have an empty pocket (even a crooked coin keeps the devil away).

"To buy a broom in May
For it sweeps all luck away."

To pass under a lean-to ladder without first crossing the middle fingers over the front ones.

"This superstition" says the *Weekly Western News,* Plymouth, "originates from an old coarse joke formerly frequent among the lower class. It took its rise from the fact that at the gallows at Tyburn the culprit had to walk up a ladder, there being no platform. The ladder was afterwards withdrawn and he was left suspended."

To break a salt-cellar.

To spill salt at the table without throwing a pinch over the left shoulder.

To help one another to salt.

To kill a robin.

To tread on a cat's tail.

To kill crickets.

To omit to inform the bees of the death of a relative, by tapping at each hive with the key of the front door. It is necessary too, to say to each hive as one taps "Maister is dead," or "Missus is dead," as the case may be.

To forget to put the bees in mourning, by placing a scrap of black crape or cloth on the top of each hive.

To forget to communicate any great social or political event to the bees. (The bees resent the omission of these ceremonies, and in consequence cease work, dwindle and die).

To give a friend a knife; as it cuts all love away.

To sneeze before breakfast.

To turn a feather-bed on Sunday.

To cut one's nails on Sunday.

To speak while the clock is striking.

To put a pair of boots on a table.

To stir the leaves in the teapot before pouring out the tea.

To have a kitten and a baby in the house together. The kitten should be sent away in order to secure good health to the baby.

To cross knives.

To kill a swallow.

To pass another person on a staircase.

To break a looking-glass, for it brings seven years of trouble, or the loss of one's best friend.

To kill a small red spider, because the insect is supposed to bring money in its track, hence it is often called the "money spider".

To begin new undertakings on a Friday.

To wash clothes on Good Friday. This must be studiously avoided to prevent any member of the family dying before the year is out.

To return, or to look back when leaving the house to start on a journey, or even when going for a short walk. If compelled to return one should sit down and rest for a few minuets before making a fresh start.

To eat any kind of fish from the head downwards, as it is against the grain.

To whistle while underground, because it will awaken the evil spirits which inhabit the caves of the earth.

To be born with a blue vein across the nose.

To decorate a house with peacock's feathers.

For a miner to meet a snail when entering a mine, as it betokens calamity, or probably the exhaustion of the lode on which he is then at work.

To see one magpie in a field, or flying across the road. Four magpies seen at one time presage death.

To reveal a child's christian name before it is presented at the font for baptism.

To receive the left hand of the bishop on the head, at confirmation. It conveys a ban instead of a blessing.

To burn bones, as it will bring pains and aches to the person who does so.

To put an umbrella on a table.

For a cock to crow at midnight, or a dog to howl between sun-set and sun-rise.

To change houses, or enter into service, on Friday.

To see a new moon through a glass window, or door, or over the left shoulder.

The advent of a comet is supposed to forebode disaster and national calamity.

An eclipse of the sun shews God's displeasure. An eclipse of the moon, that the Devil was abroad working mischief.

To see a pin and let it lie, you'll need that and hundreds more before you die.

For a child to refrain from crying when presented at the font for baptism. It is thought the more it yells and screams, the quicker the evil spirits will quit it.

For an unmarried person to be sponsor at a baptism: for "First to the font, never to the altar".

To see a coffin-ring in a candle: it shews that some member of the household, or a very near relation, will very shortly die.

For a bird to flutter against the window-panes.

For a robin to fly into a room and utter its weep! weep! weep!

For a bride to take a last peep at the mirror before starting for church.

To look back after starting on a journey. (Remember Lot's wife.)

To cut a baby's nails or hair before the child is a year old.

To look into a mirror at dusk, or night-time, unless the room is well lighted is not pleasant: for there is a dread of something uncanny peeping over the shoulder; such an apparition would portend death.

To bring into a poultry-farmer's house a small bunch of primroses when these flowers first come into bloom in the early spring. The number of chicken reared that season, are supposed to agree with the number of primroses brought in. (I once saw a little girl severely punished for this offence in South Devon).

To hear the melancholy ticking of the "Death-watch," in woodwork, is an omen of death. "Because like a watch it always cries click, then woe be to those in the house that be sick".

To see a raven hovering over a house is ominous of evil.

To take eggs from robins' or wrens' nests. Should this be done, cows feeding in the neighbourhood will yield discoloured milk, for Robin Redbreast and Jenny Wren are God Almighty's cock and hen.

To transplant parsley.

To sit down at table as one of thirteen.

To put the left foot first in starting to walk, as it indicates too much caution and brings disappointment.

For rooks to desert their rookery without any apparent reason. This forebodes ill-luck to the owners of the property. The heir will be kidnapped, or lost, and until the rooks return to their quarters, will not be brought back.

*"If thou be hurt with the horn of hart,
It brings thee to thy bier,
But tusk of boar will leeches heal,
Thereof have lesser fear."*

*"Who kills a spider,
bad luck betides her."*

To lose a mop or a broom at sea. Children bring good luck to a ship.

To whistle on board ship, as it raises storms, and enrages the devil, who in retaliation brews tempestuous weather and causes shipwrecks.

*"Save a sailor from the sea,
And he'll become your enemy."*

It is said if one's nose itches, that one will be kissed, cursed, vexed, or shake hands with a fool. To elude the three former ills one generally invites the nearest person at hand to give a friendly grip. This appears to be rather rough on the friend.

Fishermen are exceptionally superstitious and believe that ill-luck attends certain practices: for instance, they would never think of turning a craft against the sun, or of mentioning rabbits, hares, or pigs, while aboard, nor will they lend anything from one boat to another.

If the first herring brought aboard for the season is found to be a "melt," then a disastrous time in the fishing world is to be expected. If on the other hand the first brought in is a "roe," then hundreds of mease (600) will be caught and full purses the result.

Fishermen consider it most unlucky to throw a cat overboard, or to drown one at sea.

"Whoso the wren robs of its nest,
Health loses in a day;
The spoiler of the swallow's house,
Will ail and pine for aye.
And he who with his ruthless hands
Shall tear the robin's cot,
In his coffin shall have a guilty mark –
A deep red gory spot."

When unfortunate at cards you should rise from your chair, twist it round on one of its legs four times. This action is supposed to change the luck for the better.

If one's right ear gets very hot it shows that one's friends are speaking in laudatory terms of one. On the other hand, if one's left ear burns, then the friends are "picking holes in

one's jacket."
Left or right burn at night, then all things are well, both in and out of sight.

❀ Unlucky Days ❀

Certain days in each month are supposed to be unfortunate, upon which no new enterprise should be undertaken. If one makes bargain, plants or sows in the garden, or begins a journey on either of these days, misfortune will quickly follow.

"Days of evil strife and hate;
Cruel wrath and fell debate,
Planets strike and stars annoy,
Aspects, aught of good destroy,
Shun their calends,
Heed their power.
Nought begun in evil hour
E'er went well. Spirits o'er
Those days preside,
Who sport and gibe,
With human fate;
Omens of hate,
Wrath and debate."

EVIL DAYS

January 3rd, 4th, 5th, 9th and 11th. February 13th, 17th and 19th. March 13th, 15th and 16th. April 5th and 14th. May 8th and 14th. June 6th. July 16th and 19th. August 8th and 16th. September 1st, 15th and 16th. October 16th. November 15th and 16th. December 6th, 7th and 11th.

✣ CUSTOMS ✣

❈ The Hobby Horse ❈

A form of amusement popular in Devon and Cornwall is that of the Hobby Horse. This practice of assuming the forms of animals and counterfeiting their actions is of ancient date and probably formed part of the Roman Saturnalia.

The hobby horse consists of a compound figure. The head and tail of a horse, with a light wooden frame for the body (generally a couple of very slender hurdles joined at the top bars) is attached to the shoulders of a couple of strong youths, one in front with his head covered with a horse-faced mask, and another at the back who cleverly conceals his head under the frame.

The frame covered with trappings reaching to the ground hides the feet of the actors and prevents the discovery that the supposed horse has none. Thus equipped the men prance about, imitating the curvettings and motions of a horse.

As the hobby horse perambulates the streets and capers about, the village band preceding it, the children strike at it with whips and sticks; uproarious shouts of laughter rend the air, and a great deal of rough play is indulged in.

 May Day

From the time of the Roman evacuation of Britain, A.D. 410, May Day festivals have been observed throughout the country. The Saxons retained the worship of Maia, the mother of Jupiter, on the first of the month, and from this custom the month derived its name.

This popular festival was observed with the joyful ringing of bells, music, dancing, and mummings. Every building was covered with a profusion of floral decorations. Kings and queens did not object to join the members of their Court, civic dignitaries, and the populace, in the enjoyment of May Day gaieties. The makers of the fun adorned themselves with wreaths and festoons of flowers. Girls, wearing a profusion of flowers, danced around the Maypole to the wild strains of fifes and drums. Men visited the beer shops, where they imbibed more than was good for them.

As the custom grew old, abuses crept in, and what was once a picturesque and innocent recreation degenerated into frantic drunken revels, which were a scandal and a nuisance.

There were, and still are, numerous superstitions attached to the merry month of May. Marriages taking place in May are supposed to bring ill-luck to the contracting parties. Cats born in this month are regarded as unpleasant creatures to have about one, as the practice of bringing into the house snakes, toads, and other objectionable vermin is ascribed to them.

May-dew, collected before or close upon sun-rise, is looked

upon as an infallible beautifier of the complexion. Young girls arose early to wash their faces in it with the hope that their charms would be increased. On returning from the fields they would gather branches of hawthorn bloom, and suspend it over the entrance to the house, to protect it and themselves from the spells of witches and the evil eye.

On the first of May, persons were sent on ridiculous errands, and on their return, empty handed, were derisively addressed as May giize-chicks, or May goslings.

The old-fashioned demonstrations of mirth and hilarity have dwindled to feeble exhibitions of ill-dressed dolls, decked with wild flowers, carried in the hands of village children from house to house, where the occupants reward them with a few sweets or pence. Then the children sing the following words:

"Round the Maypole
Trit, trit, trot,
See what a Maypole
We have got,
Fine and gay,
Trip away,

Happy is our New May-day.
Good morning, merry gentlefolks!
We wish you a happy May;
We come to show our May garland,
Because 'tis the first of May.
Come kiss my face.
And smell my mace,
And give the little children something!"

At Helston, in Cornwall, the May-day festivals are still observed with all the old-time spirit and enthusiasm.

The Ashen Faggot

The custom of burning the yule log is observed in large country houses, at the present time, on Christmas Eve, but where the fireplaces are contracted and slow-combustion grates the vogue, small branches of green ash, are cut fresh from the plantation. These sawn into lengths the width of the grate are tied into faggots with four or five strong binds of bramble canes. Very large faggots, which are intended to be burnt in old-fashioned kitchen fireplaces, are bound with chains. The bramble binds are a source of much amusement, for soon after being placed on the dogs, they burn through, one by one. Before they begin to light and burn, each of the youngest members of the family choose a bind, and whose is first burnt through will be the first to marry. It is customary for the company to drink a quart of cider at the bursting of each bind, so that by the time the whole have given way, there has been a large consumption of that beverage. It soon begins to influence the flow of spirits and induces a hilarious state of mind, increasing in strength as the night advances.

A Harvest Custom

A VERY old custom, that of crying the neck at the end of corn harvest, still obtains in some parishes in the west of England.

When the last sheaf of wheat is cut at the end of August, the reapers take the very last handful of straw and plait the ends together, tying them with lengths of bright-coloured ribbons; then, lifting it high above their heads, wave their sickles frantically, and shout:

"We-ha-neck! we-ha-neck!
Well aplowed! well asowed!
We've areaped! and we've amowed!

Hurrah! hurrah! hurrah!
Well-a-cut well abound!
Well-a-zot upon the ground!
We-ha-neck! we-ha-neck!
Hurrah! hurrah! hurrah!"

There are many variants of the cry, but the above seems to be the one in general use. At Paignton, the farmer's name is introduced, thus:

"A-neck! a-neck! a-neck!"

"Whose neck?"

"Varmer Ferris'es! Varmer Ferris'es!
Its all a-cut!
And all abound!
And all ataken from the ground,
Hip! hip! whorrah! whorrah!"

There are some slight differences in performing the ceremony. I have seen this done in the neighbourhood of Newton Abbot, at a farm situated on the western slope of Haldon. All the reapers (between twenty and thirty) formed a semicircle, with the farmer in their midst, and the ladies of the family close at hand. The head man held the "neck" above his head, and waved it quickly to and fro, and gave the first shout of "a-neck! a-neck!"

The rest took up the cry and waved their sickles.

After this the cyder-firkin was passed round from mouth to mouth. Then a start was made for the farmer's kitchen, where a substantial supper of beef, pork, vegetables, figgy-pudden, cream, junkets, and
gallons of cyder awaited the hungry reapers. When justice had been done to the viands, tobacco and long churchwardens (clay pipes) were produced. More and much cyder at last provoked merriment and indescribable tumult. Some recounted their experiences in winter by flood, snowstorm, and hurricanes. Others their interviews with the Dowl on lonely hills, their wanderings over swampy meadows in the footsteps of Jack-o-lantern. Others their efforts to resist the evil eye, and the malignant devices of the witch. Some sung delightful old songs; and not until the daylight streamed through the diamond-shaped window-panes did they seek their beds. I should say that the wives and elder children of the men were also partakers of the harvest-supper. The neck is carried into the house and hung over the centre of the kitchen table for a year, and when replaced by the new neck it is given to the best beast in the stall.

The word a-neck is said to be derived from the Celtic language, and means "saved." Others claim for it an Irish origin, as the word "anaie" in that country means "save thou me." While another suggestion is that the custom may have been derived from the Jewish ceremonial of the wave offering mentioned in Leviticus xxiii, 10, and following verses, and introduced by the early Hebrew settlers in Britain. A long correspondence was carried on in August, 1898, in the Western Morning News, on this ceremony, from which I glean that the practice is identical in every part of the county, but there are differences in the mode of its performance.

The Divining Rod

The Divining Rod is known also as the Dowsing Rod, Moses's Rod, and the Virgula. It is simply a twig of this form V, each limb being from ten inches to twelve inches long, cut from a cherry tree, hazel, or white thorn. The operators are named dowsers, diviners, water-witches, or water-finders. Great interest is attached to the rod, as used for the purpose of discovering subterranean water-springs and lodes of ore. Its mysterious properties have been exemplified in numberless instances. The satisfactory finding of water by its aid was recently shewn at Tiverton, Plympton, Plymouth, Chumleigh, and many other places, which caused much correspondence for and against the "art" in the Western Morning News and other west country newspapers. In Cornwall, too, the dowser has pointed out spots where valuable lodes of metals have been unearthed. One case in particular may be quoted at Great Briggan, when the late Captain Trelase was the diviner.

The modus operandi is very simple, The water-witch holds the thin arms of the twig between his fingers and thumbs with the point projecting out-wards, while he walks steadily over the suspected spring or lode. If there be water or mineral below, the hazel turns upwards with a sudden jerk, if there is neither, it remains passive. It is said that the operator experiences peculiar sensations in his limbs as the twig vibrates, and that his face assumes an agitated expression. All persons are not sympathetic and the twig lies inert in their hands, but with a born dowser the rod very soon puts on vitality, and frequently completes a circle breaking short off at the points. Hundreds of persons pooh-pooh the whole thing and condemn it as a trick, and are surprised that in these days of scientific attainments people should be found weak enough to pin their faith to the virtues of a twig. Despite opposition and ridicule the search for water by this means is popular throughout Devon and her sister-counties.

✳ WEATHER LORE & ✳ WISE SAWS

The ancients observed with profound attention the natural phenomena of their time, the study of which helped them to make fairly accurate forecasts of the weather, and taught them to begin farm work and domestic affairs at the most favourable moment. They walked as it were hand in hand with nature, learning to interpret her subtle operations by marvellous intuition.

The flight of birds, the voices and actions of animals, the development of vegetation, all lent their aid to predict atmospheric changes.

Then the following traditions and proverbs were popular, and have been handed down from the earliest times:

"If Christmas Day on Monday be,
A great winter that year you'll see.
And full of winds both loud and shrill;
But in summer, truth to tell,
High winds there shall be, and strong,
Full of tempests lasting long ;
While battles they shall multiply,
And great plenty of beasts shall die.
They that be born that day, I ween,
They shall be strong each one, and keen
He shall be found that stealeth aught;
Though thou be sick, thou diest not."

If New Year's Day happen on a Saturday the winter will be mean, the summer hot, the harvest late, garden-stuff good and cheap, honey, flax, and hemp abundant.

If the weather be dry and bright on January 26th, the year will be generally of the same type. St. Paul is the guardian saint of this day.

"If the day of St. Paul be clear,
Then shall betide a happy year,
If it do chance to snow or rain,
Then shall be dear all kinds of grain,
But if the wind then be aloft,
Wars shall vex this realm full oft,
And if the clouds make dark the sky,
Both beasts and fowl this year shall die.
When midges in January play and fly,
Treasure your fodder for beasts in July."

A January spring is nothing worth.

January freezes the pot upon the fire.

If the grass grow in January, it grows the worse for it all the year. Lock your grain in the granary.

As the days lengthen so does the cold strengthen.

If the weather on Candlemas Day, February 2nd, be bright and dry, there will be a long continuance of cold wintry weather.

or,

"If Candlemas Day be dry and fair,
The half of the winter is to come, and mair,
If Candlemas Day be wet and foul,
The half of the winter is gone at yule."

or,

"If Candlemas Day be fair and bright,
Winter will have another fight,
But if Candlemas Day be clouds and rain,
Winter is gone, and will not come again."

If a storm comes on February 2nd, spring is near; but if that day be bright and clear, the spring will be late.

When drops hang on the fence on February 2nd, icicles shall hang there on March 14th.

There is always one fine week in February. When it rains in February it will be temperate all the year.

"All the months in the year curse a fine Februeer."

or,

*"If in February there be no rain,
The hay won't goody, nor the grain.
All other months of the year
Most heartily curse a fine Februeer."*

*"February fill dyke, be it black or be it white;
But if it be white, the better to like."*

If bees get out in February the next day will be rough and rainy.

When the cat in February lies in the sun, she will creep under the grate in March.

Remove all Christmas decorations before Candlemas Day.

*"Down with the rosemary and the bays,
And down with the mistletoe,
Instead of the holly now upraise
The bright green box for show."*

or,

*"If so the superstitious find,
One tiny branch just left behind,
Look ! for every leaf there may be,
So many goblins shall plague thee."*

If the eighteen last days of February be wet, and the first days of March, you'll see that the spring quarter, and the summer too, will prove to be wet, and danger will ensue.

*"February and be ye fair,
The hoggs will mend, and nothing pair ;
February and be ye foul,
The hoggs will die in the pool (Scotch)."*

If March comes in like a lion, it goes out like a lamb, and vice versa.

*"March winds and April showers,
Bring forth May flowers."*

Dust in March brings leaves and grass.

A peck of March dust is worth a king's ransom.

As many mists in March so many frosts in May.

On the first of March the crows begin to search.

The black army (fleas) arrives on March 1st.

*"Much March dust, and a shower in May,
Makes the corn green and the fields gay."*

A damp warm March will bring much harm to the farm.

Snow in March is bad for fruit and grape wine. If it does not freeze on the 10th of March, a fertile year may be expected.

When flies swarm in March, sheep come by their death.

March dust and March wind, bleach as well as Summer's sun.

March flowers make no Summer bowers.

"March borrows three days of April,
The first brings sleet,
The second brings snow, and
The third is the worst day that ever blew."

In a very old magazine I found the following, which leads one to suppose that the cuckoo arrives in March:

"In March the gükü begin'th to sarch.
In Aperal he begin'th to tell,
In May he begin'th to lay,
In July away he do fly."

A dry April is not the farmer's will.

In April wet is what the farmer would get.

Till April is dead, change not a thread.

What March does not want April brings along.

"When April blows his horn,
'Tis good for hay and corn."

On the first of April crows are still sitting.

April floods carry off frogs and their broods.

The cuckoo comes in April.

"When the cuckoo comes to the bare thorn,

Sell your cow and buy you corn;
But when he comes to the full bit,
Sell your corn and buy you sheep.
If it thunders on All Fools' Day,
There will be good crops of corn and hay."

Fogs in April foretell a failure of the wheat crop for next year.

One should look for grass in April on the top of an oak, because grass seldom springs well before the oak puts forth its leaves.

Fine warm weather from Easter to Whitsuntide produces much grass and cheap butter.

As the weather is on Ascension Day, so will it be the entire autumn.

"If it rains on Good Friday and Easter Day,
There'll be plenty of grass and a little good hay."

April and May between them make bread for all the year.

April rains for men: May for beasts.

"Button to the chin till May be in."

"Marry in May you'll rue it for aye."

No wind is colder than a May wind.

"For a warm, wet May
The parsons do pray,

*For then death-fees
Come their way."*

*"A May wet
Was never kind yet."*

*"A cold May is kindly
And fills the barn finely."
"A cold May is good for corn and hay."*

"For an East wind in May it is your duty to pray."

*"A snowstorm in May,
Brings weight to the hay."*

The more thunder in May the less there will be in August and September.

"By the first of May young crows will have flown away."

*"May, come she early, come she late,
Still she'll make the cow to quake."*

"A May flood never did good."

"Shear sheep in May you'll shear them all away."

"He who bathes in May, will soon be laid in clay."

"A swarm of bees in May is worth a stack of hay."

"In May the cuckoo sings all day."

"Change not a clout till May be out."

"Who doffs his coat on a winter's day, will gladly put it on in May."

*"A dry May and a rainy June,
Puts the farmer's pipe in tune."*

*"A misty May and a hot June,
Makes the harvest come right soon."*

"A dripping June brings all things in tune."

"A swarm of bees in June is worth a silver spoon".

Before St. John's day we pray for rain, after that we get it anyhow.

The change which takes place in the voice of the cuckoo is thus quaintly described by a sixteenth century poet:

*"In April the coo-coo can sing her song by rote,
In June oft time she cannot sing a note;
At first koo-koo! koo-koo! sings till she can do,
At last kooke-kooke-kooke; six kookes to one koo."*

If July 1st be wet and rainy, it will continue so for four weeks or more.

"He, who in July the cuckoo's voice doth hear,
Will die before he comes next year."

"A swarm of bees in July is not worth a fly."

If it rain on July 10th it will rain for seven weeks.

Ne'er trust a July sky.

All the tears St. Swithen can cry (July 15),
St. Bartlemy's mantle can dry (August 14th).

"St. Swithen's day if thou be fair,
For forty days 'twill rain na mair,
St. Swithen's day if thou be'st fine,
For forty days it will remain.
St. James' day gives oysters,
St. Swithen's day gives rain."

He who eats oysters on St. James' day will lack money to the year's end.

A shower of rain in July, when the corn begins to kern, is worth a plough of oxen, and all belonging thereto.

Very hot July, August, and September, breed hard frosts and intense cold for the next January.

If the deer rise up dry and lie down dry on St. Bullion's day (July 4th), it is a sign there will be a good goose harvest.

"Dog days bright and clear,
Portend a happy year;
But if accompanied with rain,
For better times all hopes are vain."

A heavy rainfall in the middle of July shows that St. Mary Magdalene is washing her handkerchief to go to her cousin

St. James' fair.

St. Bartholomew brings the cold dew (August 24th).

*"Dry your barley in October
Or you'll always be sober."*

Warm October, cold February. The 28th of October was anciently accounted as certain to be rainy.

*"October's brew
Will fuddle you."*

There are always nineteen dry days in October.

If October bring heavy frosts and winds, then will January and February be mild.

For every fog in October a snow in the winter, heavy or light according as fog is heavy or light.

As the weather is in October, so will it be in the next March.

Full moon in October without frost, no frost till full moon in November.

If the first snow fall on moist, soft earth, it indicates a small harvest; but if upon hard, frozen soil a good harvest the following year.

When it freezes and snows in October, January will bring mild weather; but if it is thundery, and heat-lightning prevail, the weather will resemble April in temper.

October should be a fill-dyke.

*"Crows groping greedily come back again,
With October's wind and rain."*

In December keep yourself warm, and sleep.

"The worse weather for the rider, is the better for the bider."

"If it rain on a Sunday before the mass, it will rain all the week more or less."

*"Mackerel skies and colts' tails
Make big ships carry little sails."*

*"Many a cloudy morning
Brings forth a sunny noon."*

"Leap year never brings a good sheep year."

"Hail brings frost on its tail."

"When beans are in bloom brew not your ale. When elder is white, brew and bake a peck. When elder is black, brew and bake a sack."

When the sloe-tree is white as a sheet, sow your barley whether it be dry or wet.

*"Ash before oak, there will be a soak,
Oak before ash, there will be but a splash."*

"No one so surely pays his debt

As wet to dry, and dry to wet."

"A Saturday's new moon once in seven years is once too soon."

"If the moon on a Saturday be new or full,
There always was rain and always will."

When the new moon is on her back, or shows her horns, it is a true sign of rough, boisterous weather, accompanied with heavy rain.

"Winter's thunder and summer's flood,
Bodes to old England nothing good."

"East wind and west the sign of blast,
North and south the sign of drouth."

"He who by the plough would thrive,
Himself must either hold or drive."

"When the wind is in the east,
It's neither good for man nor beast."

When the dim form of the full moon can be seen in the lap of the new moon, it is considered by some to be a sign of rain. By sailors and fishermen it is supposed to presage tempestuous weather.

"I saw the new moon late yestreen,
With the old moon in her lap:
And if we gang to sea master,
I fear some dread mishap."

When the wind is in the north, hail comes forth,
When the wind is in the west, look for a wet blast;
When the wind is in the south, the weather will be fresh and good, when the wind is in the east, cold and snow comes most.

*"Who ploughs deep while sluggards sleep,
Will have corn to sell and to keep."
"'Twixt twelve and two,
Will shew what the day will do."*

"Every wind hath its weather."

*"Autumn is wheezy, sneezy, freezy;
Winter is slippy, drippy, nippy;
Spring is showery, flowery, bowery;
Summer is hoppy, croppy, poppy."*

*"North wind brings hail,
South wind brings rain,
East winds we bewail.
West winds blow amain,
North-east wind is too cold,
South-east wind not too warm,
North-west wind is far too bold,
South-west wind doth no harm."*

*"When the wind is in the east,
The fisherman likes it the least ;
When the wind is in the west,
The fisherman likes it the best."*

"No weather is ill, if the wind be still."

"A west wind north about,
Never long holds out."

"When the wind is in the west,
Then the weather's always best."

"A western wind carries water in its hand.
A northern air brings weather fair."

"When the wind is in the south,
'Tis in the rain's mouth."

"The southern wind
Doth play the trumpet to his purposes
And, by his hollow whistling in the leaves
Foretells a tempest, and a blustering day."

Expect rain if the stalks of clover stand upright; if the flower of the convolvulus closes; if the flowers of the sorrel and of the African marigold close; if the flower of the pitcher-plant turns upside down; if the flower of the cinquefoil expands.

Fine weather is preceded by the opening of the flowers of the sorrel or the closing of the cinquefoil, and the standing erect of the flower of the pitcher-plant.

"A foot deep of rain
Will kill hay again;
But three feet of snow
Will make it come mo'."

"When hemp is ripe and ready to pull,
Then Englishman, beware of thy skull."

The sweating of stone pillars denotes rain.

✺ Signs of Rain as Predicted by ✺ the Habits of Birds and Animals

If a heron or bittern flies low, the air is becoming charged with water vapour.

When kine view the sky, stretching up their heads and snuffing the air, moist vapours are engendering, the cause of their doing so being their sensibility of the air's sudden alteration from dry to wet; and sudden rain will ensue, though at that time the sun may be shining brightly.

The chattering of swallows and their flying low about lakes and ponds denote rain.

The much croaking of frogs in the ditches and pools, &c., in the evening, foretells rain in a short time to follow.

Ants moving their eggs denotes rain, for by a secret instinct of nature finding the air changing into much moisture, they carry them to a place of drier security.

Crows flocking in large flights, holding their heads upwards as they fly, and cawing louder than usual, is a sign of rain, as is also their stalking by ponds and rivers and sprinkling themselves.

The frequent dropping and diving of waterfowl fore-shows that rain is at hand.

Peacocks crying much denotes rain.

Cattle leaving off to feed and hastening to shelter under hedges, bushes, trees, outhouses, &c., shows sudden showers are coming.

The kingfisher builds its nest in holes in the banks of a river. Should it become dislodged and float down the river and out on the surface of the sea without capsizing, then there will be a long spell of fine weather.

In some parts of the country this bird is used as a vane, not exposed to the action of the wind, but stuffed and suspended in a room by a thin string, its bill always indicating the point from which the wind blows.

"Into what corner peers the halcyon bill?
Ha ! to the east yes see how stands the wind."

"The ancients supposed that it built its nest on the ocean, and hatched its young at the winter solstice. To account for the preservation of the nest and young birds amidst the severity of the season, they imagined that the bird had a power of lulling the raging of the waves during the period of incubation; and this power was believed to reside in its song,"
So says the author of Chambers's Information for the People, vol. ii, page 447.

"The hollow winds begin to blow,
The clouds look black, the glass is low,
The soot falls down, the spaniels sleep,
The spiders from their cobwebs creep.
Last night the sun went pale to bed,

The moon in halos hid her head;
The boding shepherd heaves a sigh,
For see a rainbow spans the sky.

The walls are damp, the ditches smell,
Closed is the pink-eyed pimpernel;
Hark ! how the chairs and tables crack,
Old Betty's joints are on the rack.

Loud quack the ducks, the peacocks cry,
The distant hills are seeming nigh;
How restless are the snorting swine,
The busy flies disturb the kine.

Low o'er the grass the swallow wings,
The cricket too, how loud it sings;
Puss on the hearth with velvet paws,
Sits smoothing o'er her whiskered jaws.

Through the clear stream the fishes rise,
And nimbly catch the incautious flies;
The sheep are seen at early light,
Cropping the meads with eager bite.

Though June, the air is cold and chill,
The mellow blackbird's voice is still;
The glow-worms, numerous and bright,
Illumed the dewy dell last night.

At dusk the squalid toad was seen,
Hopping and crawling o'er the green;
The frog has lost his yellow vest,
And in a dingy suit is dressed.

The leech disturbed is newly risen,
Quite to the summit of his prison;
The whirling winds the dust obeys,
And in the rapid eddies plays.

My dog, so altered is his taste,
Quits mutton bones, on grass to feast;
And see yon rooks, how odd their flight,
They imitate the gliding kite,

Or seem precipitate to fall,
As if they felt the piercing ball.
'Twill surely rain! I see with sorrow,
Our jaunt must be put off to-morrow."

From an Almanac published 1844.

✥ RESOURCES ✥

The Publishers would like to suggest the following useful resources relating to traditional lore and folk magic in the West Country and beyond:

Legendry Dartmoor
A handy web site and bountiful resource including Dartmoor history, folklore and Witchcraft:
http://www.legendarydartmoor.co.uk

The Museum of Witchcraft
Situated in the village of Boscastle, North Cornwall, the museum houses an extensive collection of Witchcraft related artefacts and memorabilia, with many exhibits relating directly to the Craft of the West Country Witch.
http://www.museumofwitchcraft.com
The Harbour, Boscastle, Cornwall, UK, PL35 0HD

Also 'Friends of the Boscastle Museum of Witchcraft'
http://www.friendsbmw.org.uk

Contemporary Traditional Cornish Witchcraft:
http://www.cornishwitchcraft.co.uk
http://www.geocities.com/cronnekdhu
http://www.villagewisewoman.co.uk

Meyn Mamvro – A Magazine of the ancient stones, folklore and spirituality of the Cornish landscape.
http://www.meynmamvro.co.uk

51 Carn Bosavern,
St Just, Penzance,
Cornwall, UK, TR19 7QX

The Cauldron
A well established magazine of Traditional Witchcraft, magic and folklore:
http://www.the-cauldron.org.uk
M.A. Howard, BM Cauldron, London WC1N 3XX

Publishers of Traditional Ways

Specialists in folk practice, custom, tradition, lore and magic.
Visit the web site, or contact us for details of current and forthcoming titles.

www.troybooks.co.uk

Troy Books Publishing, PO Box 304
Penzance, Cornwall, TR18 9EH, England